C000010845

ESPERANCE   EN DIEU

the most imaginative modern
public garden ever created
anywhere in the world
for
the able bodied
the disabled
the elderly

and especially
for children

THE ALNWICK GARDEN

contents

THE ALNWICK GARDEN

Photo: Magi Harown

My vision
for the Gardens at Alnwick
by the
Duchess of Northumberland

I intend to revive the Gardens at Alnwick in the spirit in which they were originally made. Using the talent, expertise and technology of our time, I hope to create a place of beauty and learning which will be relevant to future generations as well as our own. Although mindful of its predecessors, it will not be a slavish recreation of the past but a garden for the twenty-first century, a contemporary, ever changing composition of sounds, sight, texture and smell. The ground plan is dominated by the movement of water. Cascades, waterfalls and fountains, waterspouts, water mazes, lakes and ponds will create ambiences to startle, soothe, delight and amaze.

THE ALNWICK
GARDEN

An artist's aerial view of the Garden proposals, showing the miriad of water courses, features, hedges, plantations and buildings, 1999.

'No gardens of this scale and ambition have been undertaken in Britain during this century. And no gardens will have quite such a magical effect on those who visit them.'

You enter the Gardens through a modest archway. Once inside, the first thing that strikes you is the sound and presence of curtains of water falling down the sides of a huge pavilion. Visible through its transparent outer skin, the building's reflection glimmers in a long, formal pool. Another glimpse through the glass will reveal a vista of fountains, terraced cascades and parterres stretching up into the distance. You will begin to register earthy plant smells and flower fragrances in the ionised air.

After this introduction, you will emerge to experience the full impact of a grand contemporary garden. Exploring its twelve acres, you discover that, just as an unassuming entrance led to the drama of the pavilion, the great garden reveals smaller, more specialised, intimate spaces. There will be, for instance, a garden for the senses, where texture, smell and sound take precedence. Other areas include a Poison Garden, a throwback to the darker side of The Middle Ages but also a practical and entertaining part of our School

Education Programme. As part of a wider educational outlook, our gardeners will be on hand at all times to help, discuss and instruct. Open paths lead into woodlands which in turn unveil a picturesque landscape with lakes and Grotto.

1   **The Cascade from the Pavilion**
2   The Serpent Garden
3   **The Spiral Garden feature**
4   The Cascade from the summit
5   **The Grass Labyrinth in Autumn**
6   The Spiral Garden
7   **The Rose Garden**
8   The Grotto
9   **The Pavilion at night**
10 The Garden for the senses
11 **The Pavilion**
12 The Pavilion at night

THE ALNWICK
GARDEN

design team

The Duchess selected the world-renowned Belgian landscape designer Jacques Wirtz and his son Peter to create the Garden; the Belgian architect Paul Robbrecht for the contemporary Pavilion.

Peter Wirtz

Born 1963, Schoten
Studies of Landscape Architecture at the Tuinbouwschool, Melle.
Since 1986 worked as a *Landscape Architect* for Wirtz
International and *Wirtz Landscape Architecture*

Paul Robbrecht

Born 1950
Partner in Paul Robbrecht and Hilde Daem, Ghent. Graduated as an Architect from Hoger Architectuur-Instituut, Sint-Lucas, Ghent 1974. Awarded Flemish Cultural prize for Architecture 1997. Recently designed the New Concert Hall in Bruges. The Alnwick Garden Pavilion is his first commission in Britain.

THE ALNWICK
GARDEN

Jacques Wirtz

Born 1924, Antwerp, Belgium

Studied Landscape Architecture and Horticulture at the Tuinbouwschool Vilvoorde

Founder of *Wirtz Landscape Architecture* and *Wirtz International*, contracting and design companies

Design of gardens and parks throughout Europe and Worldwide

Major works

Campus of the University of Antwerp, Antwerp

Cogels Park, Schoten

Bremweide Park, Antwerp

Campus Philosophy and Letters, Leuven

Gardens of the Belgian pavilion,
Osaka World Expo 1970

Emile Jacqmain Boulevard, Brussels

Carrousel Gardens, part of the Tuileries, Paris

Gardens of the Elysée Palace, Paris

Langbaanvelden social housing project, Antwerp

Camillo Torres student housing project, Leuven

Garden of the European pavilion, Tsukuba

Corporate headquarters for BMW Belgium, L'Hoist, Lens Diamond, Safinco, Barco, Maas & Co., Tabacofina, Banque de Luxembourg, Banque Générale de Luxembourg

Numerous private gardens in Belgium, Holland, Germany, Luxembourg and France

Alnwick Castle and its great park lie at the heart of some of Britain's finest scenery, and the huge castle garden forms an integral part of the landscape.

Created over three generations from the middle of the eighteenth century, the garden in its prime reflected the personal commitment and vision of successive Dukes of Northumberland and the professional skill of gardeners of the highest reputation, such as Lancelot Brown, Decimus Burton, and W.A. Nesfield. This was to become one of Britain's most admired gardens, enjoying a century of magnificence and splendour which was brought to an end by war and severe financial restraint some fifty years ago.

In seeking to recapture the lost world of this great garden, and sharing it with others, the present Duchess of Northumberland is taking up once more the innovative ideas so brilliantly demonstrated in previous generations. The proposed designs will not simply recreate the past, but also provide for a variety of educational and botanical uses needed in the century to come.

The project is a bold and ambitious one which I am delighted to support. The restored garden will be a true work of art for everyone to enjoy, and a statement both of gratitude to the past and hope for the future. I wish the project every possible success.

Charles

The Duchess of Northumberland and
HRH The Prince of Wales at the embryonic
Alnwick Garden site on 21st April 1997.

the story of Alnwick Castle

Gardens is a remarkable one

Clockwise:
Dukes of Northumberland
- I to IV

From their humble beginnings in the mid-eighteenth century the gardens had developed into one of Europe's finest by the end of the nineteenth century. Their founders, especially the first four dukes, enjoyed unrivalled reputations as men of science, patrons of botanists, collectors of exotic specimens and promoters of gardening excellence. Alnwick Castle Gardens in the North balanced the truly exceptional botanical magnificence of the dukes' conservatory gardens and grounds at Syon in the South. Proof of their early reputation rests in the visit to Alnwick of the Czar Alexander I's head gardener in the 1800s and the spiriting away of the Alnwick head gardener to Russia. An early example of international 'head-hunting'.

Of equal importance to the scale of investment and the skill of gardening technique was the inculcation in the Victorian era of the popular idea, formulated and implemented by the dukes, that the gardens should be popularly enjoyed by the general public. So the gardens became for a century a centre for popular interest and visits, made possible by the railway age.

After a final fling in the campaign of 'Digging for Victory' in the Second World War, the gardens took the full force of austere, post-war economic climate of retrenchment and were stripped to the level of barest maintenance.

Coming to the gardens in 1995 with a fresh mind and energy, the twelfth duchess visualised their one-time beauty and glory. She determined to recreate and re-invent the site incorporating the latest in water technology so they could stand once more alongside the best in Europe.

Castle, ancient town and unrivalled surrounding landscape place the gardens in a perfect setting, whose

14

THE ALNWICK
GARDEN

own beauty, tranquility and excellence in horticulture will once again arouse the popular enthusiasm and interest of a visiting public of the twenty-first century drawn from all round the world.

Attractions for the tourist of this new age are enclosed gardens, their surrounding walls replete with their original Georgian mellowness in which the fourth duke incorporated a pair of Venetian wrought iron gates which he acquired while on tour specifically for his garden restoration. On the north side of this walled enclosure will stand the pavilion which will rival its Victorian predecessor. Flanking the pavilion will be terraces and in front, stretching to the south will be a series of water gardens with gushes, spouts and fountains leading to the base of a steep mound at the South side of the garden site, down which water will wildly cascade. There will be a tea and gift shop housed within the pavilion together with conference facilities and elsewhere a point for sale of plants and shrubs, the specimens of which will be growing in the gardens. The educational role of the gardens will be particularly promoted and include specially designed programmes for parties of school children in addition to adults.

ALNWICK
GARDEN

Opposite left:
An aerial view of the Garden from the north, showing development of the Cascade and Water Basin, the Ornamental Garden to the south, Rose Garden at the west side and to the east the car parks.

heavens above!

The Garden, 1996 - still a dream.

Far right: The Tower Crane operator's view of the Cascade and lower basin under construction.

The Ornamental Garden, May 2000.

Cascade excavating for the pump room and underground reservoirs.

View to the west, 1999, awaiting the archaeologists.

View from the south showing the Garden, Castle and Capability Brown landscape beyond.

vision

Jacques Wirtz,
Louis Benech,
and the Duchess of Northumberland
inspired by the challenge ahead.

THE ALNWICK
GARDEN

to **reality**

A STORY OF CREATION

View from the Lower Basin looking up the Cascade with its twenty-one weirs.

THE ALNWICK GARDEN

19

July 97 **virgin**

THE ALNWICK
GARDEN

Triple arch into original top walled Garden.

Remains of the last conservatory.

Below right: View to the south from the site of last conservatory - now a piece of history.

Artist's impression of the Garden proposals - 1997 - showing the position of the arched gateway into the original Walled Garden at the top of the cascade, and opposite left, a view through the arch from a position at the top of the cascade.

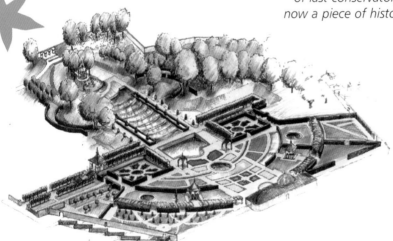

territory

The 1850 pond - used by the Percy family as a skating rink in past winters.

Archaeological survey revealed six separate levels of garden development since 1750.

ancient
April 00

Tree felling on the site of Car Park, Spring pond in foreground.

Forming new entrance on Denwick Lane.

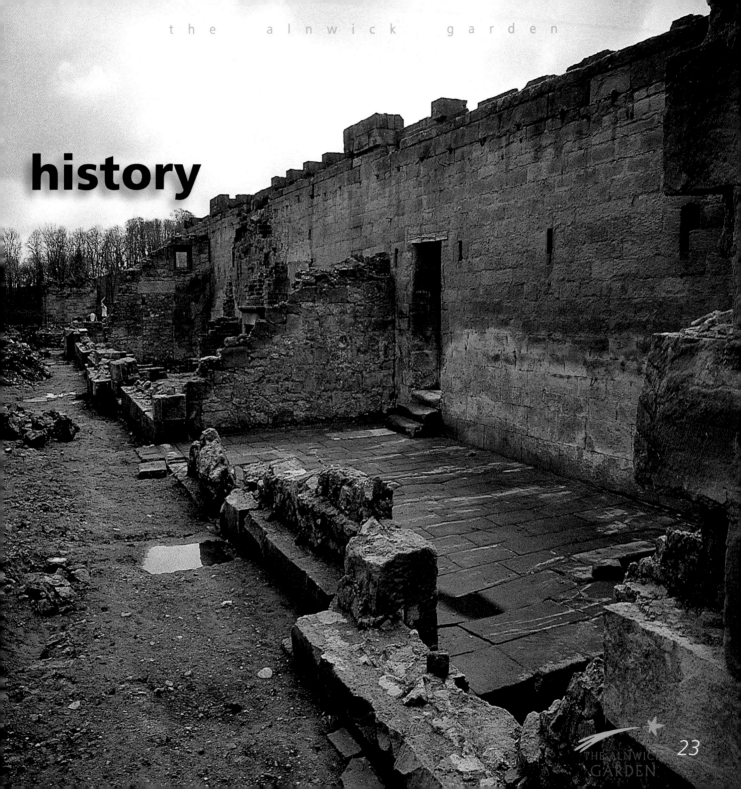

history

THE ALNWICK GARDEN

Oct 00

steps in the right direction

Above: The Ornamental Garden path construction - the first of two and a half miles within the Walled Garden.

Top: The Courtyard - formed with 88,000 Flemish paving bricks.

Above: The Site of the Pump Room B - running sand always a problem.

Top: Ornamental Garden - Beds being formed to receive 15,000 plants.

THE ALNWICK
GARDEN

Water pipes
supplying the water
features in the
Ornamental
Garden.

The 19th century
water tower beyond
the excavations.

laying the
foundations

The Tower Crane
from beneath
an arch.

THE ALNWICK
GARDEN

Nov 00

THE ALNWICK
GARDEN

Cascade under construction - Pump Room C.

cold
hard
work

Lower Basin reinforcement outlined in the snow. These areas will form the underground reservoirs to store 250,000 gallons of water required to create the water displays.

The Tower Crane at rest during the
Christmas holidays 2000 - a feature
on the skyline over the town of
Alnwick during construction works.

Will this really become the grand
garden envisaged?

29

THE ALNWICK
GARDEN

wired for action

Below: Replacing original weak wall with a reinforced retaining wall to form Serpent Garden and upper terrace.

Below: The first pleached Red Sentinal crab apples arrive - secured on their bamboo frameworks.

Above: 600 tonnes of steel reinforcement and 2500 cubic metres of concrete used to form the Cascade and Lower Basin.

Above: Pouring concrete during the construction of the source pool in the Ornamental Garden.

Above: The first arbour being erected within the Pergola.

Feb 01

THE ALNWICK GARDEN

Reception area for 850 Hornbeam (Carpinus) trees to be planted around the Cascade pergola.

Circular pool and rill - Ornamental Garden.

THE ALNWICK
GARDEN

March 01
grand scale gardening

The first flush in the Rose Garden.

coming to

Red Sentinal crab apples - the first set.

fruition

The Ornamental Garden.

Ornamental Garden arbour

16th century Italian gates.

The Rose Garden.

Aug 01

THE ALNWICK
GARDEN

THE ALNWICK GARDEN

A Final Note by the Duchess of Northumberland

I am delighted and impressed by the quality and standard of what has been created so far. However, for me this is just the beginning. My task is to raise £7m to complete the vision: a Pavilion, water, lighting, a poison garden, a grass maze, a garden for the senses, all open into the night. I want to create a spectacular venue, a theatre of water, light and music, which will leave you the visitor, spellbound, mesmerised and eager to return.

When these elements are in place I will have fulfilled what I set out to achieve and realised my dream.

Jane Northumberland

The Alnwick Garden
Alnwick Castle
Alnwick
Northumberland
NE66 1NQ

Tel: 01665 510777
Fax: 01665 510876

Registered charity no. 801959

Registered in America as
CT acct no. 0191 00616882

Visit the Garden again at:
www.alnwickgarden.com

THE ALNWICK GARDEN